BRACE YOURSELF...
THIS COULD BE FUN!

A Young Professional's Guide To An Exciting Career

Bonus: Fifty Ways to Be A Power Player

BY PAMELA J. GREEN

ISBN 10: 0988680424
EAN 13: 9780988680425
Library of Congress Control Number: 2013930596
Power Project Institute LLC, Bowie, MD

First Edition. Printed in the United States of America

Contents

"Life is either a great adventure or nothing."

—*Helen Keller*

Opening Words

Today's professional, regardless of age, must be able to successfully handle more challenges than ever before:

- Globalization
- Economic shifts
- Demographic changes to the workforce
- Information and social technology
- Legislative and governmental regulations
- Focus on the customer
- Changing talent pool

So why then all the worry about engaging young professionals? It's simple; you're different. You're just as different as the baby boomers were to the veterans and as the gen Y's were to baby boomers. Different can be scary. You bring different thoughts, ideas, behaviors, and you introduce a different way of doing things. When different enters a system of consistency and conformity (which we'll call CC), it shakes up its new environment quite a bit. When CC gets upset, it is not a pretty picture. Instead of adjusting to you, CC wants you to adjust to her, and voila another generational clash. So business leaders spend major efforts on making sure all the generations can get along just so we can get the work done, versus using that energy to address the challenges above.

You ask yourself, do I need this book? First let's define a young professional (YP) as anyone who is less than forty *and* has minimal job experience (you define minimal, please). If this defines you, then this book is for you. Someone with minimal job experience will find our approach to learning the politics of working effectively and successfully to achieve professional and personal goals enlightening. Working through systems (people, places, things) can be very challenging. This book will help you address the challenges of maneuvering through corporate politics, getting your point across, and being an effective performer. Gain the respect, credibility, and the results you desire by learning how to:

1. Make shifts in your CAB (conduct, attitude, and behavior) that get you noticed.
2. Implement five easy Power Moves that will take you from overlooked and undervalued to acknowledged, consulted, and supported.
3. Become a person of influence.
4. Use the key of resourcefulness to move you quickly to high potential status.

Still not convinced? Ask yourself if you are experiencing any of the following:

- Lack of mobility in the company because of the "pay your dues first" mentality?
- Starting to feel trapped in one role?
- Sensing that your ideas and suggestions are getting overlooked?
- Your achievement goals are clashing with company politics?
- Desire for more peer support that you do not receive?
- Comparison to other department or organizational superstars?
- Being told you're not ready for promotional opportunities?
- Uncertainty about how to move into high potential status?

Anyone who has moved up through the ranks has experienced most, if not all, of these minor setbacks and overcome them. There is a way, and this book will help you chart your own unique path to success, however *you* define it. When you are able to see beyond your current circumstances and take responsibility for your own career development, you'll see doors begin to open.

The path to success was paved by tough-minded, self-guided learners who were not afraid to stand alone in challenging situations. I'll show you how if you are willing to put the time in.

Double Your Money

"The safest way to double your money is to fold it over and put it in your pocket."
– Kin Hubbard

Canadians' debt-to-income ratio has soared to 163 percent, much higher than previously believed, according to revised Statistics Canada figures. The household debt level has increased 1.8 percent in the second quarter, bringing it to a similar level seen in the United States before the housing bust and the 2008 financial crisis (*Canadian Economist* 2012).

According to the Federal Reserve, American's are 2.4 trillion dollars in debt (approximately $7800 per man, woman, child). Also, *Business Insider* reports:

- $51 billion worth of fast food was charged to credit cards in 2006, compared to $33.2 billion the previous year.
- The average consumer carries four credit cards. The average household carries $6,500 of debt.
- 4.5 percent of cardholders are sixty or more days late in their payments.
- Roughly two to 2.5 million Americans seek the help of a credit counselor each year to avoid bankruptcy.
- In the United Kingdom:
- Every fifteen minutes and twenty-eight seconds, a property is repossessed.

- Every four minutes and thirty-two seconds, someone will be declared insolvent or bankrupt.
- Ninety-three properties are repossessed every day (based on Q4 2011 trends).

Source: www.creditaction.org.uk

How does being in debt affect our achievement of goals? Debt issues, for most people, are directly related to our lack of self-control in handling money. Show me someone who is unhappy with a job and feels stuck, and I'll show you a person who has financial struggles. The ability to properly obtain, manage, and maintain your financial resources will be your ticket to success. If you can't properly manage your finances now, early in your career, then how do you expect to finance your priorities as you move through levels of career success? The benefit of having command and control over your resources is that it creates more disposable income. The more disposable income you have, the more options you have for your future.

Self-test of your money mindset from my book *PRIORITIZE! Your Life:*

Money Mindset	True	Somewhat True	False
My bills are organized. I know when they are due and have them on a bill payment schedule.			
I pay my bills on time: therefore, I have an excellent credit score.			
I set aside money each pay for personal expenses that prevents me from mismanaging my money.			
I have and contribute to a savings account that is growing.			
I have obtained enough savings to roll over into a money market or other growth fund.			
I have saved at least 6-12 months of money to cover my expenses should I suddenly be without income.			
I properly manage the balance in my checkbook, there are no surprises.			
I pay off credit card balances whenever possible, monthly if I can.			
If I must, I have one – no more than two - credit cards for personal expenses.			
When I don't have the cash for a purchase, I am more likely to wait to make that purchase than to place it on a credit card.			

8-10 True   Great job! Clearly you are ready for the next level.
5-8 True   Not bad. Some work needed, but you're on your way.
0-5 True   Consider speaking with a financial planner or accountant for assistance.

The goal of this exercise is to make you more aware of how a positive money mindset looks and what you should be shooting toward, if you are not there yet. Consider it your money mindset checklist. A lower outcome doesn't mean you can't achieve your goals, but it will help you see where you can begin to make improvements.

Remember, money doesn't automatically secure your future, and having it doesn't automatically create options—only *you* can create viable options by properly managing your resources and planning how you will utilize them to guarantee your future success:

1. Speak with someone you trust who is handling his or her finances reasonably well to help you collect names of reputable financial advisors. If your employer has a financial management program through its retirement program (most do these days), then check it out.
2. Make contact with and interview these individuals to determine if they will be a good fit for you, and then select one to work with.
3. Read, read, read books and resources on money management.
4. Be prepared to start saving money. Start small and gradually give your retirement savings a raise.
5. Establish a budget and follow it. Discipline yourself to stick to your budget. If you can't establish self-control over your finances, you'll find it very difficult (if not impossible) to accomplish your goals.
6. Stay abreast of the progress with your finances and with your financial advisor. Become a student of money management.

You're bound to find yourself in challenging jobs. Don't use your resources as a jailbreak opportunity to leave a really horrible boss; use it to finance training and education to move you upward and onward—and of course that one-time jailbreak when the company won't deal with a really bad leader!

JOHN MACGYVER VS. EDWARD CULLEN

[lahy-k*uh*-b*uh*l]
(Likeable)

"Would you like you, if you met you?"
— *Tegan and Sara*

Angus MacGyver was the lead character of an American action-adventure television series named MacGyver that ran for several seasons in the United States and on various other networks abroad from the late 80's to early 90's.

The show follows a secret agent who used very creative and imaginative strategies to solve complex challenges with seemingly anything he could find. Refusing to handle a gun, his Swiss Army knife and duct tape were premiered in every solution he came up with.

Then there is Edward Cullen, a fictional character in Stephenie Meyer's *Twilight* series. Edward is a telepathic Vampire who, during the course of the series, falls in love with, marries, and has a child with a human teenager who later chooses to become a vampire as well.

Some might say a matchup between the two is no matchup at all—they are from different eras and have different skill sets, and the younger Cullen would win hands down. Others might say, age is not a factor, but experience is, and the wisdom of MacGyver's experience and his resourcefulness would make him a winning opponent.

Clearly each has an admirable skill set that makes for a worthy opponent. But what if they were on the same side, the same team, both using their skills to advance a united effort as opposed to fighting one another? This is the basic issue facing many people in the workforce today. It isn't that we don't each bring admirable skills and expertise to the table; it's that we allow our personalities, biases, and other issues to get in the way of productivity.

Life is certainly no joke, but sometimes we need to learn to relax and enjoy the ride. Who wants to do that alone? Working life is tough enough, but trying to go it alone as a superhero, if you will, is even tougher. Being a likeable person who can get along with others will give you the opportunity to become a positive influence on someone else because people want to be around likeable people. If you posses the skills of either of the heroes above but walk with a shoulder load of arrogance, your capabilities will be shut down, and no one will be able to see you showcase your best talents!

Find Common Ground

Learn quickly how to establish a connection with people, a connection that is genuine and sincere. You will then see less resistance to you personally and professionally. Finding common ground is as simple as learning more about what you have in common than that which you do not. MacGyver and Cullen come from very different backgrounds, generations, and experiences, but the one thing they have in common is their skillful ability to defeat the bad guy.

Let's be perfectly clear—some people won't like you, as one coach put it to me, "simply because they just don't like you." Most of the time you'll be able to recognize them immediately, through the way you are treated and the things they say to you and about you. Only you can determine if the relationship is worth pursuing to raise your likeability rating in their eyes. If, for example, your boss is a MacGyver figure, accustomed to the traditional way of doing things, and resents you for whatever reason, then that is probably a relationship worth pursuing and improving. Why? Your superhero powers with his or her superhero powers can do wonders. Don't pit yourself against someone in leadership if at all possible. Look for ways to make your superhero powers work in partnership with his or hers.

If, on the other hand, the person is less significant in your opinion, he or she might still be important to your success; you should still try to address the situation. If this person is unwilling, then let it go, but don't allow it to hinder your own productivity. To pursue everyone whom you feel doesn't like you can become tiring and frustrating. It can also make you appear needy, and in such cases, you lose friends and influence because you are tiring someone else out with your need to be liked.

In the book *The Likeability Factor: How to Boost Your L-Factor and Achieve Your Life's Dreams*, Tim Sanders points out:

> Life is a series of popularity contests. The choices other people make about you determine your health, wealth, and happiness. And decades of research prove that people choose who they like. They vote for them, they buy from them, they marry them, and they spend precious time with them (Sanders 2005).

How many job opportunities, promotions, and other experiences were you denied simply because you did not connect with the decision makers?

I grew up with a mother and father who used to tout the phrases "You get more bees with honey than with vinegar." and "Attitude determines altitude!" Sometimes we make it so easy for people to say no or to deny us an opportunity because we approach the situation already defeated or with too much pride and arrogance. Living with these two extreme attitudes is begging for failure. So what can you do? How do you know if your attitude is holding you back? If you are unsure if your attitude is holding you back, consider:

- How well do you get along with others?
- Are you most often sought after for advice or for the latest gossip?
- If you were to conduct a 360-degree survey of everyone you work with—I mean everyone and not just the people you believe will assess you favorably—would the outcome about your attitude be more positive or negative?
- When you think about promotional opportunities, would you want to be led by you? Why or why not?
- Are you more of a peacemaker or a troublemaker?
- Would a survey of your peers and co-workers reveal you were more or less respectful of people? In other words, do you or do you not treat people with actual or perceived higher position, power, authority, or status more favorably than those without power, position, authority, or status?

Getting in the Right CAB

The CAB you drive determines how far you can go. Think of this metaphorically, as if you had the choice between two CABs:

CAB A:Clean, neat, smells fresh, friendly driver, car in good shape, with no dents or scratches

CAB B: Dirty, smells of cigarette smoke, disheveled grumpy driver, car looks like it has been in several accidents, perhaps only moments ago

Even if you had to pay a little more, most people would leap to CAB A. This is symbolic of your:

Conduct

Attitude

Behavior

Though both CABs can get you there, you want it to be a comfortable and enjoyable ride. This same holds true of those with whom you work. If your attitude stinks, you snap at people, your personal life is headline news day in and out, you only have time for you, you lack discretion, have poor communication and interpersonal skills, and just seem out of control, you are not going very far in your CAB.

So how do you clean it up? There are at least five steps:

Step One: Assess Your Super Powers

What strengths, capabilities, skills, and experiences do you bring to the table that might make you appealing to an employer in your line of work? In what ways might you be able to team your super powers with others?

Step Two: Find Common Ground.

Where have you found you've been in most conflict with others? At what point was there a clash? Was it over ideas, suggestions, etc.?

How might you find common ground to have better control over the situation when it presents itself?

Step Three: Reality Check

Make a list of how you want to be viewed; then have your own reality check of how you are really viewed. For example:

Super Power Projection: How I want to be viewed	Current Reality: How I'm current viewed
Creative	Unimaginative
Resourceful	Prosaic
Self-assured	Low-self Esteem, Morale
Confident	Poor Self Image, Low Self Confidence
Collaborative	Contradictory
Genuine	Apathetic
Responsible and Reliable	Immature, unreliable
Resourceful	Indecisive, indifferent

Your Turn

Image Projection	Current Reality

If you struggle with any of this, you'll need to enlist the help of your friends, family members, co-workers, and your boss (current or former). Ask them:

- When you think about my conduct, attitude, and behavior, can you tell me something positive and something I need to work on? (Note: Do *not* let them off the hook on things you need to work on. People who really care about your future will be honest. This means you have to create room for them to do so. If they are afraid to be honest, then you have your answer.)
- In your opinion, what is my greatest strength?
- What do you find most interesting about me?

We have a complete set of free resources to help you conduct a more thorough self assessment: www.powerprojectinstitute.com/resources/.

Step Four: The Assessment

Assess what help you'll need to achieve your projected image. Some people might only need a mentor; others might want to secure a professional coach, and still others might need to work with a licensed health care professional to address issues that are a little more severe. There are some who will need to work with all three.

Remember, this is about being the type of person other people *want* to be around. If you can't make that happen, then achieving other career goals, even if you want to remain a thriving performer right where you are, could be threatened because people want to work with people they like. We spend too much time at work not enjoying the people around us.

Step Five: Commit to change.

Find a person who will hold you accountable for your goals. For some, making changes in their CAB will be extremely difficult. This isn't about being fake; people will see through that. What you will be required to do is show sustainable improvement. People will comment; some won't be quite so nice when you change. Others have to adjust to the new you, and they may not like that. So if you are prone to making foul comments or using inappropriate language and decide that you are going to stop—guess what—someone else is going to do his or her best to make you fail, over and over. Your job is to resist that temptation and work at maintaining a positive attitude and outlook. Strive to be worthy of respect by peers and leaders.

Power Up!

What did you find most useful in this chapter?

_____

_____

How can you position yourself to be more of the type of person people want to be around, without compromising yourself, your values, and your beliefs?

_____

_____

STRATEGY 2

UNDERDOG TO THE RESCUE!

[per-**fawr**-m*uh*ns]
(Performance)

"If I had some duct tape, I could fix that."
—*MacGyver*

Underdog was an underestimated mutt who people disregarded because he didn't look like a ferocious beast who could fly, save lives, or even be scary. However, when given the chance to perform, he jumped (forgive the pun) at the opportunity.

Jean-Dominique Bauby is a real life underdog. On December 8, 1995, at the age of 43, Bauby suffered a massive stroke. He found he was entirely speechless when he woke up twenty days later with only the ability to blink his left eyelid. Bauby's entire body, including his mouth, were paralyzed. Despite his tragic condition, he wrote the book *The Diving Bell and the Butterfly* by blinking when the correct letter was reached by a person who would slowly recite to him the alphabet. Bauby composed and edited the book one letter at a time. The book was published in France on March 6, 1997 and Bauby died 2 days after the French publication of his book.

Regardless of the situation life presents, or the tools, skills, and abilities you have or missed out on, companies are looking for performers who are resourceful, determined, and committed. These are the people who are tapped for leadership—people who are unafraid to pursue excellence and who are willing to find a way to get results.

Within your career, your personality and your performance are the two things that are within your complete control. Fail in these two areas, and you'll find that the roadblocks to career success are your own doing, not anyone else's. Your mindset drives your behavior, just as it did with Bauby. What is your mindset at work? Place a check mark next to the one that most resembles you today:

Group 1:   Up and Comer

You feel fortunate to have landed a good job with this company so early in your career and have decided that you don't want to leave anytime soon. You want to grow with the company. You'll definitely become a vested employee and win longevity awards if properly engaged. You are a high potential performer with lots to offer, and you offer as much as you can when the opportunity presents itself.

Group 2:   Passing Through

You like the company, but see it as a stepping-stone to other career opportunities. This will be a company that will not only add value to your resume, but that has the potential to enhance your business acumen. Your tenure with the company will likely be between three to five years. Your energy, enthusiasm, and passion make you stand out among peers, but you are really trying to get on that fast track to success.

Group 3:   Sentenced

Perhaps due to the skill deficiencies or challenges with your CAB, you are not finding the type of success you need and are having difficulty finding work elsewhere. This could also be the result of working under a really bad boss for a period of time. Your lack of engagement could lead you to be seriously detached, which could also lead to performance challenges. Your performance is average year to year, and sometimes dips below average.

Group 4:   Satisfied

You are not necessarily looking to move up, but you are interested in remaining challenged in your role. A shift that makes you feel less than engaged in a significant way could push you to the *Passing Through* or the *Sentenced* categories. If the company properly engages you, you will be a key driver of business success. You maintain an above-average performance rating.

Of course there are varying shades of gray to these categories, and it is not only possible but realistic to find success and failure with each of the categories above, depending on how you define success. These categories speak more to the attitude of the performer and his/her approach to work and less to the actual skill of the person. If someone is a committed performer, he or she can find success with the right attitude and a good fit with the company.

Ensuring the sustainability of your organization's future is not just the CEO's job. Everyone should be on the lookout for future opportunities and the negative implications of business decisions or the absence of sound judgment. Ensuring sustainability may mean introducing your company to something new. Leaders get ahead of change; they don't just follow it. So how can you improve your performance in a place, even if the company doesn't have the ability or maybe even the willingness to finance it? What will be your approach to obstacles you face on the road to success? What if you are challenged to resolve an issue, solve a problem, or find a solution to a serious business matter?

Want the keys to being resourceful? Here they are: S.O.L.V.E. I.T.

S = Study the Problem:

- What is the issue at hand?
- What situation am I trying to resolve?
- What are the possible causes of the problem?
- Who was involved in the events leading to the problem? How might they be helpful?

O = Organize the Facts:

- What are the facts I need to take into consideration?
- What pieces of information will be most useful?
- What historical pieces of information do I need to gather?
- What do I know to be true about this situation?

L = Line Up a Plan

- Research the possible solutions. What have competitors done (or are doing)?
- What experiences do I have that can add value?
- Who in my network can help, provide insight or guidance?
- Is there a blue ocean opportunity that exists?
- Identify and prepare the top three solutions.
- Create scenarios around each solution.

V = Verify Your Plan with Others

- Determine who needs to be informed and consulted.
- Who is ultimately accountable for the outcome? What role is he or she playing?
- Who will make the final decision?
- Who is responsible for various aspects of the outcome? Do they know their roles?
- Has everyone done his or her part to ensure a successful outcome?
- Is there anything that is not ready?
- Have I garnered the support I need from internal sponsors?
- Am I prepared to address opposing arguments?

E = Examine Your Options

- Do my recommendations make sense?
- Do my recommendations adequately address the original problem?
- Are my options reasonable, achievable, measurable, realistic, relevant, and do they meet within a reasonable time frame?
- Is there sufficient buy-in for the options to be implemented?

I = Inform Key Stakeholders

- Have I chosen the appropriate reporting method for my recommendation?
  - Full report of findings to executive leaders and other key stakeholders.
  - Fact sheet to those who need to be informed or were consulted.

- Talking points to higher-level management and those peripherally involved.
- Verbal presentation to all key audiences.

T = Take Action

- Choose the solution.
- Carry out my plan.
- Examine and report on results.

When Mistakes Happen

One way to peer into a person's character is to see how he or she handles mistakes. We are all prone to mistakes, some of us more than others. It is not enough to clean up a mistake, or even to own up to it—though both can be viewed as honorable. So what should you do if you find you've made a mistake, no matter how big or small?

1. Assess if the mistake needs to be made known to a broader audience, such as a boss, teammate, or superior before it is addressed. If the mistake will affect further work processes, then make it known, and address it immediately. If it is a minor error that will not affect further or broader work processes, then perhaps cleaning up the mistake, making a mental note, and not repeating it is good enough.
2. Own up to it. Humbling ourselves when we must admit to mistakes makes others less likely to pound us with harsh punishment. Humbling oneself is not a way to get out of a mistake; it shows responsibility for a mistake, regardless of the punishment.
3. Resolve it. Examine what went wrong—not to lay blame, but to ensure you don't follow the same path in the exact same way.
4. Determine the possible solutions, not just the quick fix—which could lead to a bigger or more complex set of problems. Be prepared to think quickly about the possible solutions that you can report to your supervisor or to your team.
5. Involve the suggestions and ideas of others. If it is a team issue, then consider bringing the team in immediately to help resolve it. If you have time, consider speaking with your coach or mentor about how you might address the challenge.

6. Implement the solution or resolution as quickly as possible and make note of what you've learned as a result. The mistake was not an exercise in how to properly cover your behind, but it was an opportunity for learning. What did you learn about yourself and about others? How might you apply that learning to your next project?

7. Build community. Avoid laying blame, pointing your finger, or otherwise shifting responsibility to someone else when problems arise. When you build trust among teammates, peers, leaders, direct reports, and others, you will get tapped for more opportunities.

The key to being seen as a resourceful professional is taking responsibility for the good and the bad in your performance. It is difficult to be a leader when no one is willing to follow you. Additionally, it is difficult to get tapped for cool assignments when others are reluctant to work with you. What type of work environment are you creating?

Power Up!

What did you find most useful in this chapter?

_____

_____

Is your performance really where it needs to be? How do you plan to take it to the next level?

_____

_____

Apply the S.O.L.V.E. I.T. technique to a problem you are facing—make note of the reaction of those around you!

_____

_____

ARE YOU SMARTER THAN A FIFTH GRADER?

[pee-*puh*l]
(People)

"If you would win a man to your cause, first convince him
that you are his sincere friend"
—*Abraham Lincoln*

When Gabrielle J. Williams graduated from the fifth grade in Bowie, Maryland, she had written a book, was CEO of a successful jewelry company, and spoken to hundreds of girls around the country. Here's what Gabrielle wrote in her first book, *The Making of a Young Entrepreneur* (comments in brackets are by the author):

WARNING: DREAM KILLERS!

People will always hate on you, but you can't let them get to you. Not everyone will support your dreams and goals. It's important that you don't let these people make you think any less of your dreams. These people are dream killers. A dream killer is someone who tries to make you doubt your dreams.

It is important to surround yourself with people who believe in you and who will not be dream killers. Make sure you know who your dream killers are so you can avoid them as much as possible. Sometimes, you can't avoid them—especially in school [at work too]. You might have a dream killer on your bus [project team] or in your class. Even some teachers [leaders] can be dream killers. When you have dream killers around you, avoid telling them your business. If they don't know what you're doing, they can't say anything bad about it. (Williams 2011, 28)

Working with People

There are many careers where working with people on a daily basis is rare. But even though rare in those instances, when the occasion presents itself to hold a conversation with a human being, make sure you can build relationships, meet a need, and address a problem in a professional manner.

I was speaking at a conference one day, and in the middle of my talk, one lady said quite appropriately in response to a statement I'd made, "Where there are people, there are bound to be problems." Let's face it; we will not like every one we meet, work with, or encounter. There will be customers who make you feel as though you are going insane. There will be immediate supervisors and leaders who will make you scratch your head in wonder as to how they were able to attain certain levels of leadership. When these moments present themselves, it is a signal for you to get ready to shine—to put on a mask, as a friend of mine told me once, and pull that mask so hard it feels you can't breathe, and just deal with it. The other person has to feel you are genuinely concerned and not that you are being fake or phony, because people can see right through phony behavior.

So how do you convey concern and interest for a Dream Killer whom you don't really care for or whom you know really doesn't care for you? It's easy; you become an Academy-Award-winning actor or actress for that moment. I'm talking Meryl Streep acting, not *Sesame Street* acting. Meryl Streep can play any role to perfection. She can play a dumpy housewife, magazine mogul, a British prime minister, and a Texan to perfection. In each role, for the moment, she lives that persona. There is no magic pill here. Figure out a way to do what needs to be done to get through the moment or period of time needed to be successful. Let me warn you, this will not be easy. When your emotions get involved and you internalize things said or done, dealing with people who are not likeable or who don't seem to "get" you can be one of the toughest things you face because, in most cases, you will need people to get the work done.

If that doesn't work, remember people want to be given respect. If you can, find a way to show genuine respect for the work, even if you don't care for the worker and you may find it much easier to make it through tough interactions.

Not everyone needs to know every emotion you are feeling or every thought you are having at every moment you are experiencing them!

C'mon, it feels good to let loose one good time, but those are traps of our ego saying, "Feed me. Feed me, please." Don't fall into that trap; it is a deep pit that is difficult to pull out of. Check the ego, and focus on the work. If someone is really a challenge, then you need to work through HR. No one should suffer abuse from a customer, client, co-worker, or leader. The other thing to keep in mind is that people have a way of helping to sharpen your sword. If you never learn to effectively deal with difficult people, you'll always be caught off guard by challenging behavior.

The Key to Great Interactions:

- Communicate with respect. Show respect whenever possible—you'd want that even if *you* were having a bad moment.
- Be willing to help. A helpful attitude can transform someone else's.
- Find a way to say yes. People are so used to *no*; find a way to help them if it is at all within your power to do so.
- Assume positive intent. There may be a backstory that you have not been made aware of; get the details before jumping to conclusions.
- Give your undivided attention. Put away the cell phones and tablets, and take your eyes off of the computer. Physically give your full attention to the person with whom you are speaking.
- Be inclusive in conversation, social interactions, and business dealings. If others are standing around, don't ignore them, draw them in to the conversation; make them feel their presence is important.
- Take notes. When appropriate write down important facts to help you with total recall later. Ask the speaker, "Do you mind if I take notes or write this down?"

Building Social Capital

Social capital refers to the value of the relationships you have in your network. As Power Networking Guru George Fraser once said, "Someday your network will be worth more than your net worth." Becoming a social butterfly and fluttering around to every networking event in the city is not what I am referring to. This is about building meaningful relationships with individuals who add value to you personally and professionally and vice versa.

When I am asked for someone who can create a website, design logos, deliver customized training on a particular topic, or consult in an area of expertise, I have my finger on at least one person in my network who I can use as a referral. Not only am I building value with the person I am referring, but also with the person I am helping. The other tip I'd offer is to ask people, "How can *I* help *you?*" Then, help them when they respond. Most will not lay a request on you; others, though, may keep that in mind and come to you later. Having a helpful attitude will pay high dividends to the account owner.

Power Up!

What did you find most useful in this chapter that will help make working with you more engaging?

_____

_____

Create a resource list of people with businesses, skills, expertise that your network might find helpful; include websites, apps, books, and other useful information, and share often.

_____

_____

Identify someone you've had challenges with at work and create a plan to improve that relationship within the next few weeks or months. How will you knock his or her socks off?

_____

_____

CRYING DOESN'T HELP. IT ONLY TELLS THE ENEMY WHERE YOU ARE.

You have to learn the rules of the game. And then you
have to play better than anyone else.
—*Albert Einstein*

I'm Just Doing My Job:

*In December 2012, the UK News Website Mirror reported a traffic
warden was branded a "heartless Scrooge" after ticketing ambulances
collecting disabled kids from a charity carol concert.*

*The over-zealous warden slapped tickets on the vehicles as they
collected wheelchair-bound children. Stunned onlookers took snaps
of the council worker as he ticketed the ambulances in Nottingham
on Monday.*

*He refused to stop issuing the fines even as the disabled youngsters,
from a local school, were being wheeled aboard. The warden then
swaggered away from the scene after slapping two £70 penalty notices
on the vehicles.*

*The incident took place after 12 kids from Oak Field School and
Sports College had performed in a lunchtime carol concert. A pair
of ambulances parked in a loading bay to let the children board the
vehicles when they were spotted by the warden.*

*Despite onlookers begging the warden to show leniency, he refused to
back down - telling them: "I'm just doing my job" (Mirror News
2012).*

Stories like this are all too common, when someone takes his or her job
so seriously that common sense takes a backseat. However, rules, policies,
and procedures are put in place to govern behavior, and unfortunately the
fear of repercussion leaves some employees feeling they have no other

recourse than to "do their jobs!" This man may have been recently written up for violating a policy or received a mandate that during the holiday season there would be those who try to take advantage of the "system.". Perhaps, even, he had seen someone else reprimanded for doing the "right" thing, even though they may have bent the rules a little. We may never know, but these are the types of things that cloud our judgment and perhaps clouded his.

Do you think the over-zealous warden probably wanted to cry after reading this story? Yeah, maybe.

I'm not advocating breaking all the rules, but you should know which ones are more pliable than others. If you want to let those who might not be your fans know what your weaknesses are, just wander through your day without a clear understanding of policies and procedures for basic functionality within your work environment. They will find you. If you make a conscious decision to bend the rules, try to clear it first with superiors or follow up with them immediately afterward and have a darn good explanation for making the call. You might get one pass for the sake of customer service, company reputation, saving a sale, but it may not happen again.

Policies and procedures are those written rules created for your success. Learn them, and become highly functional; don't and you will trip over your own feet time after time.

Who or what is influencing your thinking?

The things we see, read, and hear all influence our thinking. The conversations we hold, the programs we watch, the meetings we are in influence how we think. It is important to capture and recognize what influences our thinking because it shows up in our conversation, in our writing, and in our CAB. As professionals, we must be careful to take nutritional sustenance into our minds in the same manner that we feed our bodies.

If you want to position yourself for leadership opportunities, you must be cognizant of what leaders expect of someone in the position you seek to obtain. This is similar to the notion of "dressing for the job you want, not the one you have." Feed your mind with positive and productive conversations; seek insight into business decisions. Read related business magazines and network with progressive people. Newsflash: people who aren't going anywhere don't want you to go anywhere. You may have to find new lunch buddies if you want to improve your thinking. You'll need people you can converse with to balance and shape your thoughts. We sharpen one another's swords by engaging in conversation. Pick up a book or two on a business topic of interest.

Finally, cut out as much mental junk food as possible. Sure, find some time to veg out once or twice a week, but if your daily routine is an eight-hour day at work followed by a long, intimate evening in front of the television, you have a lot of opportunity waiting for you. Use your newfound time to develop and implement some of the strategies that you're learning about in this journal.

John C. Maxwell and co-author Jim Dornan, in their book *Becoming a Person of Influence*, write that influential people possess key characteristics: They have integrity. They nurture other people. They are good listeners. They seek to understand people and help them grow and develop. They help them navigate their personal and career paths. They empower those around them, and they seek to reproduce other influencers. The authors describe stages to becoming a person of influence by the following steps:

Modeling: Becoming the person you want to see in others. People may not remember what you said, but they will remember how you made them feel. What behaviors or qualities are you modeling before others?

Motivating: Connecting with people in a positive way on an emotional level. Helping to build people's self-confidence and positively affecting their self-worth and self-image will lead them to allow you to influence their conduct, attitude, and behavior.

Mentoring: Maxwell and Dornan's third level of influence. Mentoring is a verb, and verbs are an expression of *action*. Thus a mentor is a person who regularly engages in the act of being a wise and trusted teacher and supporter. Mentoring calls for mutual agreement that the relationship is one of teacher and student. Understanding the meaning of mentoring is important because many individuals in leadership positions consider themselves mentors to subordinate staff, with no correlating action to support their notion of being a mentor. True mentors can track the results of their influence in the life of a mentee, and the mentee can then attest to the influence of the mentor relationship. If you consider yourself a mentor, yet the mentee's life is not being positively affected, improved, and visibly changed by the relationship, I challenge you to consider if you are in fact a mentor or just a friend.

The fourth and final level of being an influencer according to Maxwell and Dornan is the notion of **Multiplying.** These authors contend that in order to attain this highest level of influence, you must "help people you're influencing to become positive influences in the lives of others and pass on not only what they have received from you, but also what they have learned and gleaned on their own." How unselfish and generous one must be to achieve this level of influence.

Who are you influencing?

Observing all that drive in you are people who see *you* as their lodestar, even if they never convey this to you. Everything you say and everything you do is being observed both intentionally and unintentionally. Some people will seek to observe and report only on the negative things they see and interpret in your behavior. These people would never admit that even they are being influenced by you, even if it is only subliminally. When you challenge people to think differently about a person, place, thing, situation, problem, or opportunity, you are in essence saying to them that what they currently think is not correct. It's human nature to not want to admit when we are wrong, so these people would rather challenge you than readily change their own minds. It is that simple and that true.

If more people would acknowledge that to get something new, they have to change the way they think, we'd probably be building that Tower of Babel talked about in the book of Genesis. Don't let someone's critique of you eat you alive. It is just another form of feedback, and actually, it is a compliment because they are really saying, "You are challenging me to think differently, and I don't like it." You can't possibly please everyone, and not everyone is going to love you, but you can seek to establish and maintain a relationship that allows you to influence the behavior of others. How do you do this? Well, not by arm wrestling people in to submission. You do it by speaking the truth in love, not getting overwhelmed by negativity, picking your battles carefully, holding your position in the face of opposition, and seeking to create win-win situations whenever possible.

Power Up!

What did you find most useful in this chapter?

_____

_____

Are there rules and regulations, policies and procedures you don't quite understand? How might you get clarification on those immediately?

_____

_____

Are there policies and procedures that you think might need an update? Are there policies and procedures that interfere with customer service? Who might you approach at work to make your case for creative or innovative changes?

_____

_____

STRATEGY 5

THE BOSS'S JOKES ARE ALWAYS FUNNY

• •

[pol-i-tiks]
(Politics)

"The person who knows 'How' will always have a job. The person who knows 'Why' will always be his boss."
—Diane Ravitch

The Board Prayer

I worked as the director of human resources for a large not-for-profit organization at the time of this occurrence. The board chair at the time was not a fan of the current CEO, who was public about being agnostic. During a board meeting, the board chair looked at me sitting in what we called the 'choir seats' (chairs positioned on the outskirts of the room for the company directors to sit) and said, 'Pam, would you please open us up with prayer?' After getting a wink of approval from the CEO, I obliged and said a very short prayer and returned quickly to my seat, while the board chair boasted a proud look of triumph on his face. It was the first and last time anyone ever prayed at a board meeting. I was neither fired, nor reprimanded, as the CEO recognized I was a pawn in a game of chess between himself and the board chair.

The feeling of being put on the spot, of being used, and being tested is one of the most depressing and thrilling experiences you could have at one time. On one hand you feel worthy of being tested, of being picked out among all the other beautiful swans in the room, but on the other hand, there is fear that perhaps there is some sinister joke being played on you. In the situation above, I knew clearly that the board chair was pushing the CEO's buttons and that I was being used to push harder. My peers were floored by his request and all stated that they could *not* have stepped up to the plate if asked—so they said. Perhaps that is why I was chosen. Who knows, but what I knew was that the CEO was very level headed and would not reprimand me whatsoever. He found it amusing and went about his work. I'd say that while the point was made that the chair was in control, the CEO proved his ability to be unflappable in the midst of warfare.

But what if the CEO were not level headed and would not have been so understanding? My decision could have been quite different. In hindsight, I believe I had three choices:

Option A: Do as the board chair requested and deal with the CEO's failure to understand later.

Option B: Get the approving glance from the CEO and then proceed to do as requested.

Option C: Run!

Without the CEO's approving glance, I was familiar enough with the board to know there were several ministers in the room, and I would have asked respectfully for one of them to pray on my behalf. I also know that if the CEO would not have given his approval, *he* would have spoken up immediately, which is what I believe the board chair was hoping for. In any case, that quick glance at the CEO was a life saver.

Politics are the sometimes spoken, but mostly unspoken, rules of how things get done in any environment. In the context of the work environment, politics operate at every level and at cross levels as well. The key is to recognize that they exist and to learn some swift maneuvers of your own. You will have some wins and some real losses throughout your career. You may be experiencing them right now, but there is a way to work through the political quagmire that exists in your organization.

The first is to decide how you want to position yourself. How do you want to be viewed by leaders and staff within the organization? Revisit the chart that you completed in *Strategy One*. If you want to be viewed as honest and direct, as a person who gives respect and learns how to maneuver through systems effectively, then you will need to demonstrate these behaviors and characteristics repeatedly and unapologetically. Regardless of how you choose to be viewed, the moment you falter or your character and behavior shows a different and unappealing side of you, your audience will judge. Some will judge more harshly than others, but you will be judged.

Having a momentarily lapse in judgment or being flappable when you should not have been are things that happen to the best. Stop, breathe, think, and then decide. You may decide to act; you may decide to do nothing at all. Take the situation above: the CEO could have jumped up and showed his disapproval of the board chair's request, or he could have reprimanded me for following through, or he could have done any number of things to show his disapproval. But he stopped, took many deep breaths, thought about where he was and who was pushing his buttons, and by judging his "opponent" well and reading the tone and mood of the audience of about twenty other board members and ten staff, he made the best decision for the moment. He recognized immediately that he was being tested, and he passed simply because he didn't flinch, grimace, or grunt and he respected the wishes of his board chair.

Most situations, and I could name a few, will be much more severe, but remember: Stop. Breathe. Think. Decide—that is all you need to do. When you get into action, think, *Will the action make me feel better?* or *Will the action I take make a meaningful difference?* If it comes down to you just feeling better that you acted or responded to a situation, perhaps you need to keep breathing. There will be times you will need to take a stance, and those are times to be calculating and thoughtful. When you must take a stance, choose your words and your tone carefully, and never do so in writing. Remember the fictional character Jerry Maguire? His manifesto cost him his job and almost ruined him.

You are going to encounter good and not-so-good work environments, most of which are dictated by leadership. Under good leadership you will flourish; under bad leadership you will dry up like a prune.

> *"There are two kinds of people, those who do the work and those who take the credit. Try to be in the first group; there is less competition there."*
> —Indira Gandhi

Maneuvering Corporate Politics

Maneuvering through corporate politics requires many things. Knowing your level of influence with leadership and managing it well tops the list.

Why is influence so important in corporate politics? As we discussed in *Strategy 4*, you should be concerned about the impression you are making on three groups of people in your work environment. There are others, but these pose the greatest threat to your success:

- Your immediate supervisor
- Your work team
- Your circle of trust (those who have your back) at work

People who are successfully maneuvering corporate politics recognize how important is to have others help them stay informed about what is going on in the organization. This isn't about gossip; it is about knowing what the undercurrents are that make or break the cycle of progress in the organization.

Riding in your CAB is your reputation, professional capabilities, work experience, demeanor, expression of thought, physical and mental posture, and likeability. No one loads these in to your CAB but you. You control them all, and no one but you is responsible for how your CAB looks when it pulls up to the door of your job every day. Want to influence your altitude? Change CABs.

The external factor you face riding in your CAB is not about what you can't control, but about what you can influence. No, you can't control how people think, what they do, or even what they say, but you can influence all of them. Someone may have some deep-seated reason for disliking you or people like you for reasons beyond your control; your job is not to change his or her mind but to put your best foot forward in everything you do. Interaction with you alone will challenge that person's thinking, which will eventually change his or her mind.

These things don't happen overnight. You don't buy a person coffee one day, and then, snap, just like that, they like you and want to help you in your career. It takes time for him or her to repeatedly see consistently positive conduct, attitude, and behavior in you that makes the impact and thus the change. It can take six days, six weeks, six months, or six years for influence to take full effect. Be patient, and don't lose hope. Change what you can about what is riding in your CAB and watch how far you can go.

Create Win-Win Situations

Creating win-win situations is about how you make people feel, especially in difficult or adversarial situations. As Abraham Lincoln said, "Nearly all men can stand adversity, but if you want to test a man's character, give him power." As a professional, you are in the driver's seat most of the time, especially when it comes to decisions about human capital. You have the power to make a situation better or worse. What will you do with that power? Will you use it to benefit someone else, or will you wield it like a giant sling?

Say yes to new ideas and experiences. I'll never forget the first time I worked in a secretarial role. I had aced all my high school typing and clerical tests and was typing about one hundred wpm when I graduated. I knew everything. Then I went to work in an office and was asked to set up some additional files. I looked at the current system. I hadn't seen it before, so I knew it was wrong and decided I would do things "right." After all, it was the 80s—this system must have been outdated. Wrong. I hadn't seen this system for filing because I had never been exposed to it. I didn't ask questions, and when corrected by an office manager, I was somewhat offended. She tried to get me to understand the purpose for setting up the files and folders in that manner, and once I listened, it exposed me to an extremely efficient way of filing.

From there, I looked for new things to learn in every environment. I adopted the mantra that I'd try almost anything at least once. When asked by a different employer to help coordinate a company golf outing, I said yes. I hated the idea of golf and being on a course, but I said yes because I had limited exposure to fundraising. From there I was asked to help with another event, to which I said yes. Did I get extra money, title change, or special acknowledgement? No. But I benefited significantly from the knowledge and experience gained, which helped me as a business owner.

In every job situation, learn something new. Learn a new skill, competency, or way of looking at things. This will build your skill set. In the end, you could find that you're one of the most valued employees in the company.

There *are* situations when a no answer is the best answer, and you'll know when those times present themselves. In making your decision, consider:

- Is there a way this offer could help me grow personally or professionally? If so, in what ways?
- Are there any potential setbacks, or is there a downside to taking on this responsibility or opportunity?
- How might I leverage this opportunity for my future?
- Am I learning something new?
- Is this moving me in the direction I wish to take my career?
- How will this affect my reputation and credibility?
- How was the decision made to invite me to take on the role or responsibility?
- Is it a temporary or permanent assignment?
- What's in it for me, from the point of view of the person extending the offer? (What does he or she see in me that I might have overlooked?)
- Am I compromising my morals or ethics in any way?
- Is it illegal, harmful, or in any way potentially damaging?

The answers to these and other questions will help you determine if the new opportunity or experience being presented is the right opportunity for you. Keep in mind that not every *offer* is an *opportunity* for you. Assess each situation separately, and make a decision that is best for the company but also best for you and your career.

The Power of Silence

When used appropriately silence can give the appearance that you are wise beyond your years, and when used inappropriately, it can send the unintended signal that you are intimated or afraid to speak up. So when does one use silence appropriately?

- When you are in a coaching conversation and want someone else to come to a conclusion for himself or herself.
- When someone has said something so ridiculous that only silence will allow his or her words to reverberate back to this person and smack him or her in the face, even though you want to.

- When you know you can't win an argument.
- When you've said all you can and you still do not feel you are being heard.
- When you need to take a moment to think about how you might offer thoughtful insight into a conversation or discussion taking place.
- To avoid or bring closure to an unproductive conversation.

Silence is often used when a person feels too timid to speak up or when he or she has been so harmed by someone, usually a superior, that he or she uses silence to mask hurt. In cases where you have been publicly disrespected, and every case is different, privately and immediately following the incident, make it clear you did not appreciate the way you were spoken to and ask that it not happen in the future:

"John, I want to speak with you for a minute about what just happened. I would like to ask that if there is an issue you have with me personally, that you take it up with me in private. I felt disrespected by how you spoke to me and would appreciate being spoken to in a manner of respect. The same respect I give you."

Have a tone and demeanor that conveys sincerity, respect, and seriousness. Don't joke it away, and don't say it is "OK," because it is not. Also, don't end the conversation with a joke or levity. If you are serious, you want to end the conversation by leaving the person in quiet self-consultation. Also, don't mix it into the middle of another conversation; this can weaken the seriousness of the situation. Gracefully make your exit, and don't bring it up again.

The worst thing you can do is publicly become unraveled. Have you considered that the other person might be trying to push your buttons just to discredit you? Don't give anyone the keys to your emotions by "losing it;" if he or she wants to win the argument, give it to him or her, especially if the person in question is a superior staff person. There will be other opportunities to make your case.

Power Up!

What did you find most useful in this chapter?

_____

_____

Rate yourself on the corporate politics scale (1—I need work through 5—I'm a master of my domain). How do you know? Are there elements of your CAB that get in the way?

_____

_____

What makes you a valuable performer? How might you showcase your value more consistently in new and creative ways?

_____

_____

JESUS IS COMING! EVERYBODY, LOOK BUSY!

[ri-zuhltz]
(Results)

"Too many companies believe people are interchangeable. Truly gifted people never are. They have unique talents. Such people cannot be forced into roles they are not suited for, nor should they be. Effective leaders allow great people to do the work they were born to do."
— *Warren Bennis, Organizing Genius:*
The Secrets of Creative Collaboration

Thomas Alva Edison is one of the most famous of American inventors. Edison was responsible for making many of the modern conveniences we now enjoy including night lights, movies, telephones, records and CDs.

The first electric light bulb is Edison's most famous invention. Edison was responsible for inventing and improving things that dramatically changed our world. Whether he inventing things alone or with others, almost all are still being used in some form today, inventions that just about everyone and anyone could use.

Someone once asked Edison about the secret to his success in which he replied, "Genius is hard work, stick-to-itiveness, and common sense".

When a leader, supervisor, or important person walks by, we rush to look busy to give the appearance that we are producing results. Why is that? Truth is there are some leaders who just don't like to see employees socializing at work. It really bothers them. I worked for an older woman once who felt that there was just too much laughter, which was a signal that employees weren't working hard enough. Yeah, seriously. This way of thinking still exists, and I have news for you, even some young people have these opinions. However, there is one thing you can do to combat this way of thinking...

Producing results is critical for all of us in business. It is not so much about you, though many of our reward systems make you believe it is. As with Edison, it really is about producing something everyone, a broader audience, can use. Whether you work for someone else or for yourself, results determine the value of your contribution to the company. When you go to work anywhere, you'll want to know how your performance will be measured, what are the expectations, and then you can blow it out the water. Exceed expectations at all costs.

Making a Business Case

Top business leaders recognize that there are too many options and too many choices available to employees, customers, clients, and consumers in general when it comes to how they spend their time, their money, and their energy. If you want to be in the top class of professionals, you must recognize the importance of this key point.

Technological advances are creating new opportunities and introducing more competitors at a rapid rate. These technological advances and rapid growth in direct competition are eating away market share and eating in to revenue of businesses across the world. Top business leaders recognize that the buffet of technological advances being made available to consumers means that customer loyalty will come at a premium. This type of competition has sparked the focus on corporate social sustainability and responsibility, growth in customer loyalty programs, and public relations campaigns designed to capture the heart and mind of consumers who increasingly are doing business with those organizations that are socially responsible, who pay attention to their individual needs, and whom they know, respect, and trust.

How can you present a compelling business case to your supervisor, especially in the wake of a tough economy, declining revenues, and organizational challenges? If your organization does not have a process for implementing new ideas, here is a five-step process for making the pitch:

Recognize the Dilemma

The situation might be crystal clear to you, but business leaders, given a choice, are going to focus on what they believe is most critical and threatening to the business. Who could blame them? If two vehicles are coming toward you, and both pose a threat, you're going to avoid the one likely to have the most damaging effect. Business leaders will often see the technology threat as a semitruck driving downhill at 65 mph, and a social media threat as a ten-speed bike. The key is to not overexaggerate the threat. Make the issue relevant and don't make the business leader pick. Don't make this an either/or situation. Once you recognize that all the other business disciplines are projecting and forecasting too, your job is to then help him or her see how addressing the social media threat will prevent that semitruck from getting out of control.

Crystallize the Business Opportunity

Define and articulate the exact problem or challenge that faces the organization:

1. Why is it a problem? Is it because of legislative or governmental changes?
2. Has your organization made changes to its strategy?
3. Have there been commercial developments in the marketplace that pose a threat?
4. Is there another employer moving into the area that could siphon talent?
5. When did you recognize it was an issue?
6. What are the implications if it is not resolved?
7. What is the timeframe for addressing and bringing resolution?
8. How much of an investment and what type of investment will it require?
9. What supportive data can you offer to help your case? This includes financial implications, research, and your own analysis. Also, historical data analysis of your organization's performance (employee surveys, trend analysis, workforce analysis) is a good source for predicting future performance. Spend time at the library—yes, they still exist—with a librarian who will help you identify the resources you'll need to build your case.

Suggest Alternative Solutions

After crystallizing the opportunity, you'll need to present alternative solutions to your immediate supervisor, if not the CEO. There will be a number of solutions you could select; however, your job is now to narrow the number of solutions to those that yield the greatest return. An example of how you might lay it out would be:

Summarize the Business Challenge:		
Describe Solutions	Pro's	Con's
Solution A		
Solution B		
Solution C		

Ensure you forecast the costs and risks associated with implementation of each solution.

Recommend a Preferred Solution

The solution you recommend for implementation should be the one you believe will bring about the greatest benefit to the future of the organization. You'll need to define why you are recommending this particular solution. Don't focus on the lowest cost to implement. You want to focus on the greatest return for your investment, and in some cases, it may cost more to get what you are seeking. If these are employee-related costs, speak in terms of investment, not just expense. In your outline of your preferred solution, make sure you address:

- Your implementation timeline and communication strategy
- If there will be a need to establish a project team, who would be asked to serve, the role of the team in the planning process, and expected time commitment
- The measures of success: What does success look like and how will you know it was a success? What measures will you put in place to evaluate progress over time?

Gain Buy-in and Support

This is the opportunity to work both within and across functions and departments, especially stakeholders, to discuss your idea. This responsibility to obtain buy-in and support may need to come at the genesis of your idea, once research is complete and you are forming your recommendation. In other organizations, it may need to come at the end, once you've "sold" the idea to your immediate supervisor, if not the CEO. Be cognizant of internal culture and politics when establishing a business case, and respect your culture. Bottom line: if you don't know, just ask.

Business thought says:

- How do we make money?
- What is our business model?
- What are our key performance indicators?
- When the economy shifts, where do we likely see positive growth or diminishing returns?
- When was the last time we conducted an environmental scan? What did it tell us? What did we learn, and did we make adjustments to the business accordingly? Why or why not?
- Are we regularly discussing the external factors affecting our business?
- What scenario plans are in place, and who is monitoring them?
- If I scan the lists of companies that have won awards or are recognized for their business management practices, innovation, financial stability and growth, employee engagement, etc., what things do they have in common? Are we on that list? Why or why not?
- What is our reputation?
- Is the process flow in our organization helping us to become more efficient and effective? Who is monitoring the process flow for our organization? How do the outcomes compare against our forecasts and performance indicators?
- How are workflow interruptions, such as absenteeism, silos, mistakes, and rework, affecting the business? How do we avoid and prevent these types of interruptions?
- Who are our competitors? Who is keeping an eye on them?

This list is not exhaustive; however, you can use these questions as starting points to shape your thinking about your company. Being strategic and being viewed as strategic are dependent on the questions you ask and the things you do. Just asking these questions and pontificating publicly about what you think no more lends credibility to you as a leader than to know the reasons for a problem and never speak up to offer the solution. Timing and articulation are critical to being influential in your organization.

Moving forward in your career requires a realistic look at your skills, capabilities, and strengths to bring about the greatest job satisfaction, marketability, transfer of skills, and income potential for you and your family. So, where have you been, what have you done, and how well did you perform?

Moving to the Next Level

To take your career to the next level, a critical step is to explore and come to terms with your source of motivation. Change for change's sake without personal purpose and meaning could lead to a life filled with unhappiness. Going to the next level in your career may require you to change, take some risks, travel, speak publicly, or develop other skills or competencies. In a global world, your career possibilities may seem virtually limitless; however, only you know your limitations. Consider your motivations for moving forward and check only three:

❑ Greater authority or leadership role

❑ Autonomy in my work

❑ Business-related travel

❑ Responsibility for supervising people

❑ No responsibility for supervising people

❑ Opportunity to capitalize on my creativity

- ❑ More job security (tired of threat of layoff in this line of work)

- ❑ More money (want to maximize my income potential)

- ❑ Balance between work and family (overtime is not an option)

- ❑ Greater prestige and visibility

- ❑ More of a set daily routine (I like the consistency of knowing what I'll be doing from day to day with minimal change)

- ❑ Variety of tasks on a regular basis (I like a lot of change)

- ❑ Team-oriented work

- ❑ Work from home most days of the week

- ❑ Flexibility and freedom from a routine work schedule

- ❑ Other preferences:

If you are ready for the next level, you must not only be willing to expand and change, but you must be able to function well as a good corporate citizen. Think about it: most people will be working for someone else until retirement. If you think being a business owner is an escape clause, think again. Even business owners are accountable to boards and their customers. You never escape having someone to report to. Being able to work successfully in an environment controlled by someone else is critical.

Power Up!
What did you find most useful in this chapter?

In what areas of business acumen are you a rock star?

_____

_____

What other areas might need your attention as you progress in your career?

_____

_____

POOR PEOPLE HAVE BIG TV. RICH PEOPLE HAVE BIG LIBRARY.

—Jim Rohn

[**prog**-res, -r*uh*s *or, esp. British,* **proh**-gres; pr*uh*-**gres**]

(Progress)

In order to succeed, your desire for success should
be greater than your fear of failure.
Bill Cosby

A young girl from Kosciusko, Mississippi always believed she was destined to be someone great. Oprah Winfrey learned early on "to turn misery into wisdom" as she would later state. Her misery included being raised on a pig farm with no running water; being sexually abused by a family friend and later by her own relative; and at the young age of 14, giving birth to a baby that died a week later. Indeed, by the age of 14, Oprah had experienced more misery than most of us could imagine.

Eventually she received the discipline she needed to turn her life around. Not only did she grow academically, she would later win a scholarship to Tennessee State University where she would study broadcast communication and get a part time job as a reporter on a Nashville television station. This lead to Oprah's continued growth to become the first African American broadcaster in Nashville.

Oprah then landed a most prestigious job opportunity with a Baltimore broadcasting station. A larger market where mistakes were rarely tolerated, Oprah found that correcting her mistakes would not be enough to save her broadcasting job. Her apparent attitude and appearance on camera proved not to be a good fit and though she wasn't fired, she was given a lower paying position as a daytime talk show for a program that appealed to local housewives titled "People Are Talking".

...and the rest is history.

A progressive person never gives up—though he or she wants to from time to time, this person just doesn't. Like Oprah, he or she experiences many setbacks along the way. If we borrow a much-quoted saying by Willey Jolley, "A setback is a setup for a comeback," Sometimes, as in the case with Oprah, we walk right into our destiny, and in other times, it seems so far off that it is unrecognizable.

To be successful as a twenty-first-century professional, it will take a combination of all of the things you've learned in the preceding six strategies. Clearly those things, your CAB, your chosen business environment, and the business expectations of the company you work for are all ingredients in your success. None of them can work solo. They work in concert with who you are becoming. Some organizations are clearly more progressive than others, so a leading-edge, twenty-first-century professional in one organization might look vastly different from another, and both could still be considered progressive and successful in their own rights.

How Big is Your Library?

If you want to make gigantic leaps forward, fill your library of the essential knowledge, skills, and abilities needed to succeed in your chosen line of work.

A. First Build a Core Set of Competencies:

Business Savvy:

Full comprehension of your profession, as acquired through a combination of education and work experience. You consistently stay abreast of key trends, professional changes, and appliCABle laws, rules, and regulations, as well as recognizing their various applications in the work environment when needed.

Customer-Centric Behavior:

Focus on and understanding of the changing needs of the customer. You ensure that the organization fosters a customer-centric culture.

Business Focus:

Understanding of the needs of the business and industry.

- Read the annual report and other business reports published by the organization.
- Take a business course in the area of business in which you need the most development.
- Conduct and maintain a competitive analysis of your organization's competitors for talent and product or service line, and share your findings with key internal stakeholders.
- Pick a business unit for which you have little knowledge or exposure, and work with them to solve a business challenge.

Innovative and Creative Orientation:

An eye toward the future and implications for the business and the organization. You demonstrate the ability to establish plans to meet implied projections.

Tactical and Strategic Capability:

Understanding of the difference between being tactical and being strategic. You can adjust performance and interaction to play each role interchangeably when needed. You can quickly distinguish when you need to act in either role.

Adeptness in Information and Social Technology:

Being adequately attuned to technological advances that affect the work world and using technology to achieve organizational success. You stay on top of and incorporate social media strategies whenever appropriate.

Believability, Trustworthiness, and Credibility:

Establishing and maintaining a culture of trust and credibility. You seek to exceed expectations of the internal customer and support the philosophy of exceptional internal customer focus and service.

Career Self-Management:

Taking responsibility for your own career. You know what you like, where you are strong, and areas for improvement. You readily take on assignments that challenge your knowledge base and establish career benchmarks that you monitor.

Courageousness:

Having an edge—the willingness to take on assignments, try new strategies, and test concepts that the average person in your position might not. You are capable of standing on your own in the face of opposition and possess a sense of fearlessness that gets you noticed and respected. You maintain composure and are unflappable when faced with setbacks or defeat.

B. Business Savvy Professional

Becoming business world and industry savvy is as easy as reading important magazines and periodicals such as:

- National and global business magazines, like *Forbes*, *Harvard Business Review*
- Online resources, including *Barron's* http://www.barrons.com; *Hispanic Business* http://www.hispanicbusiness.com; *Wall Street Journal*; http://wsj.com; and *Bloomberg* http://www.bloomberg.com

Don't run out and get the book of the week, but do pay attention to what leaders are reading and what is toping the best sellers charts as it relates to your core business and your own development. Still, it is important to build your own library of resources. To help commit something to your memory, make time to share or discuss it with others. Gently slide it into normal conversation, rather than make the conversation about how much you think you know. Introduce it in a "matter-of-fact" kind of way. For example, "Wow, that makes me think of an article I read in *Forbes* recently about…Has anyone read it yet? If not I will forward it to you. It was really very timely."

Don't forget that current affairs may also mean that you demonstrate that you have personal interests outside of work. If you have a favorite television program, sports team, or hobby, you should feel free to introduce it into light conversation when appropriate. It makes you appear less of a robot who is only looking to get ahead and more like a normal person who has a life beyond the office. Please, have a life outside of work.

Thrive at Work

As a young professional, you can flourish in your job, and although weird might be the new norm in popular culture, it may not necessarily be the new norm in the predominately traditional work environment of today. Organizations with "cool" cultures like SAS, Zappos, Abercrombie & Fitch, and others who offer the opportunity to Rollerblade on campus, wear casual clothing, and so forth, still require you to meet and exceed the requirements of your job. Those who are offered cool assignments, job enrichment opportunities, and promotions are those who ***consistently*** go above and beyond in their job and who can work across cultural and organizational barriers. You're facing the experiences of multiple generations at work, from those who firmly believe you need to earn your place at the top (and even those who believe young people should be seen and not heard) to your generation of fast-paced doers.

You might ask, "How do I do that without seeming to be an overachiever and alienating my peers and others in the organization?" The answer is easier for me to convey than for you to do. At some point, young professionals will have to learn to break away from the pack without alienating them. This doesn't mean abandon your fellow lunch buddies, but it does mean broaden your network and organizational exposure.

As a leader, I can promote only one person at a time. Rarely are multiple promotional opportunities available within a department in short periods. In promotional situations, supervisors are looking for individuals who can, with help, manage the politics of going from peer to supervisor while developing and executing operational and strategic goals. Going from peer to supervisor is best done when you have already established credibility with your peers. Those *not* ready for leadership opportunities tend to exhibit these kinds of behaviors:

- Repeatedly agreeing with and following the decisions of the crowd, even to their own detriment
- As a peer, repeatedly turning to the crowd to help make decisions that affect their own work
- Having a reputation for getting overly involved in watercooler discussions and as a regular contributor to the gossip ring
- Bonding with the less reputable employees at work
- Lacking control of their emotions in situations that affect them or others they care about
- Offering feedback to others or in work scenarios that is perceived as more destructive than constructive

These are just some of the ways in which you can be derailed early in your career. Avoiding these situations requires you to establish productive and supportive work relationships. Observing and taking note of the way work gets done in your organization and how the more respected and accomplished leaders in your organization find success will be key to how well you thrive. Take note and remain in constant self-improvement mode.

Lastly, adopt an attitude of exceptional customer service. Seek to create win-win scenarios for even the worst customer interactions and respond in a timely fashion and with a good attitude when someone reaches out to you for assistance. People will always remember how you made them feel. In this customer-driven society in which we live, the ability to obtain and maintain customer loyalty and engagement (internal and external) will get you noticed.

Take Control of Your Career

Make a Plan:
Where do you see yourself in the next three to five years? What role can/will this company play in this plan? What knowledge, skills, and abilities

will you need to achieve your goals? What areas of your conduct, attitude, and behavior need to improve? Are there areas of competencies that need closer attention?

Write Your Vision:

This is your roadmap for staying focused. Where do you want to take your life and your career?

Design Your Strategy:

What steps will you take to move toward your goals? What scholarship programs or grant money might be available? What is available that is free? If your company won't pay for the development, might they pick up partial expenses, such as travel or registration fees?

Believe:

You have the capability to produce results and get other believers to support you emotionally and financially too. Believe that you have what it takes to succeed. If you don't believe in yourself, who else will?

Take Action:

How will you get there and what tools and resources will assist you? Meet with others who are in your line of work or where you're headed. Through these conversations, you can research and strategize what actions might be of greatest benefit to you.

Plan Your Exit:

How you leave your job is just as critical as how you start a new job. The business world is both large and small at the same time. Even if you aren't well connected in the local business network, it is likely that someone you have worked with is well connected. The purpose for establishing these connections is to gain access to information that might not be otherwise available to the average person. For example, most companies today have policies that prevent offering references, but you really don't believe that there is no way someone can obtain a reference on your past performance—do you? As a young professional, you ought to be building a solid reputation, one of credibility and trust among other things. People are ten times more likely to communicate negative information than positive. This means one mistake could follow you well into the future. Here's some advice:

- Give notice inside the stated policy. If no policy is given, then offer at least a two-week notice. If in a leadership role, the rule of thumb is thirty days.
- Communicate in private with your immediate supervisor and then offer a written notice.
- If a counteroffer is extended, consider it over a reasonable time frame (a few days) and promptly get back to your employer with your answer. If you decline the offer, send a written letter that acknowledges and thanks them for thinking of you in such a way that they would extend a counteroffer; explain that you believe the move you are making is the best one for you at this time in your career.
- Never speak negatively about the employer with co-workers or future employers.
- Stay away from negativity about your past, present, or future employers in social media networks, because, as the saying goes, you can't unring a bell.
- Finish pending assignments, and ask for guidance for establishing priorities to close out projects. Don't slack off.
- Ask for a written letter of reference from your immediate supervisor and secure it before you leave.
- Leave a letter to your successor helping locate key files and giving insight into the systems and processes you have in place.
- Keep a copy of things you've created or make note of systems and programs you've implemented to add to your career portfolio. It is often impossible to obtain copies once you've left your employer. While you may not be able to claim ownership of intellectual property (resources created for or on the behalf of the employer), you can certainly take credit.

These are just some things that will help you make a proper exit from your current employer when the time comes. Thinking in terms of legacy building in your exit will help you stay focused. Sometimes, leaving is tough, but when the leaving is easy and you can't wait to get out, still adhere to this advice and be thankful you're leaving. Don't give anyone a reason to say something negative about you.

Sometimes, as a young professional, it will seem you are doing all the right things—building relationships, establishing credibility, improving yourself personally and professionally—and still you constantly run into roadblocks, especially those put up by other people. This is frustrating. But think back on the things you've endured thus far in your life. It is usually those tough lessons and experiences that you have learned the most from. I have endured some very tough situations and some really strange leaders throughout my career, but in the end, I learned more than how not to be like them; I learned how to improve myself! I was strengthened as a result of going through the challenge.

You will be challenged even when you do the right thing; just keep moving forward. Do not let your performance suffer because of other people. If nothing else, make sure your performance remains on point, regardless of what is going on around you.

Power Up!

What did you find most useful in this chapter?

_____

_____

What aspects of your "library" might need to be expanded or enhanced?

_____

_____

Poor people have big TV. Rich people have big library.

What part of Oprah's story did you find most inspiring?

_____

_____

What is your story? How will you make it exciting?

_____

_____

Your Seven Power Moves!

Five strategies, plus two bonus moves, that can take you from overlooked and undervalued to acknowledged, consulted, and supported!

This book has thoroughly discussed each of these in greater detail; however, it is up to you to apply what you have learned, and you can begin to do so immediately. The first two are totally within your control: personality and performance. How you perform here will determine how your company chooses to engage you. Your goal is to prove yourself worthy of retention to your company. With limited amounts of dollars to spend on employee retention, development, and training, companies are increasingly selective about whom they choose as investments. Will it be you?

Here they are:

Within Your Complete Control		
(1) Personality		(2) Performance
Are you someone people want to work with?		Does your performance consistently exceed expectations?
Within Your Company's Control		
(3) People	(4) Policies	(5) Politics
How well do you get along with others? How well are you mastering the art of building relationships?	What are the written rules you must know to meet basic performance standards?	Are you successfully maneuvering the spoken and unspoken rules of engagement?
Bonus Decisions for You and Your Supervisor		
(6) Progress		(7) Pull-Out
After feedback, are you stepping up to the plate and giving your best performance? Are you bringing your "A" game to the table? If so, are there promotional opportunities or further development programs that are open for you?		Is it time to move on either because you've gone as far as you can or you find that this isn't a good fit after all?

When you look at this chart, you'll see that you really can't change that middle layer. It is the place where you are responsible for adjusting to the company and the culture. This period of adjustment can be uncomfortable, but there is no reason for you to just give up and quit. It is in this period of adjustment that you learn more about yourself than you ever thought possible. One thing you can count on is that everything in that middle layer is bound to change over time—some things slower than others, but they will change, even if slightly.

We can't always have input into the people we work with or for, the policies that are created and enforced, nor the politics or culture under which the company runs. That feeling of being "sandwiched in" has real meaning here. If anything in that middle layer is off as it relates to you specifically, even slightly, your performance, reputation, and level of engagement are at stake. You can adjust, and most people do, given time. You can try to fight the system, and well, in rare instances that can work as well, but only rarely. You could also make a decision to move on. Only remember this: that middle layer exists everywhere. Every company has its own brand of craziness; it is just a matter of what brand you are willing to choose. Choose wisely, and when you do, add value!

Bonus: Fifty Ways to be a POWER Player

1. Be innovative. Being innovative means taking something that exists and making it different and better or introducing something entirely new.
2. Be a person of influence
3. Create win-win outcomes
4. Conduct your skill gap analysis. What skills are required to be an efficient performer? What skills do you have, and what is missing?
5. Get focused. Stay focused.
6. Assess your business acumen. The business world changes every minute of the day. Are you keeping up with the requirements of the new demands that face your business? This knowledge will help you stay relevant and build your credibility as a business leader and professional.
7. Get needed training and development. Explore and define the type of training and development you need to achieve your career goals. Will training courses meet your development needs, or will you need to pursue a degree program?
8. Seek counsel and support. Who have you included in your circle of advisors? Do you have a mentor or coach? Who is providing you with guidance through your career and work-related decisions? Securing wise counsel will help you as you move throughout your career.

9. Obtain feedback. We all need feedback. It helps us know if we are headed in the right direction, assimilating without losing our brand identity, and where exactly we need to correct our course. It is also the way in which we build relationships and obtain positive information about things we're doing well. Obtain feedback on the completion of every major project or career turn. Don't wait until an annual review—lots of information gets lost in that timeframe.

10. Implement. What plans or ideas are you holding on to that you need to release? What classes do you need to take? What applications need to be completed? What books or articles need to be written? What certifications are you waiting to secure? Get these things on your timetable and launch them.

11. Achieve organizational alignment. One of the best ways to ensure career growth is by determining where your company is headed and then identifying opportunities to build your skills along with the growth of the company.

12. Dress professionally. Sometimes dressing for the part you want isn't appropriate for the job you have. Your dress isn't the only thing to get you noticed; your personality and performance certainly will, but make sure you dress according to professional standards for the job you have.

13. Build your professional network by connecting virtually and in person.

14. Join a professional association for your career, and get involved.

15. Create and rehearse your introduction or "elevator speech" to introduce yourself when networking.

16. Build your voCABulary. Speak the King's English when you need to, and use slang only when it is appropriate outside work.

17. Recognize there are some people who just aren't going to like you just because they don't like you. Focus on building relationships on the team and off the team. Don't focus on being a people pleaser so much as a relationship builder.

18. Remember you are a company representative on and off the job.

19. Do what you say you're going to do.

20. Follow up with people in a timely manner.

21. Support final decisions, even those you don't agree with.

22. Keep confidences. Knowing the importance of confidentiality and how to properly safeguard confidential information is essential. Something as simple as keeping confidential paperwork concealed, turning it over when it's not being used, is critical in this age of information and identity theft.
23. Make commitments and establish policies that will benefit others.
24. Build a reputation for doing the right thing.
25. Weed out the poor performers when it is within your power to do so.
26. Excel at communication in speaking, writing, and body language.
27. Come out of your office—talk with people, and become a great listener.
28. Keep a gallon jar of candy (the good stuff) on your desk—it says, "Come in; I don't bite!"
29. Be clear on the expectations of your job. Review your job description with your supervisor when you first start and repeat annually during your performance review discussion.
30. Read your favorite business- and career-related publications.
31. Apply something you've learned to the work you do to complete the assignment; offer something new to the organization, or enhance an expected outcome.
32. Keep track of your accomplishments.
33. Develop and maintain good boss and peer relationships.
34. Seek professional development at an appropriate pace: trying to do too much too soon could be intimidating to longer-tenured employees and thus create unnecessary roadblocks as a result. Also, longer-tenured employees may be offered development opportunities ahead of you.
35. Clearly understand work assignments, and make no assumptions in completing them.
36. Ask questions until you are confident that you understand what is expected of you.
37. Avoid being overly apologetic. If you say, "I'm sorry," when your dog accidently bumps into you, you've got some work to do. If you apologize too often, what is the likelihood you'll soon be awarded blame, even when it isn't warranted?
38. Get help as soon as you need it.

39. Develop a keen understanding of the needs of your internal and external customers, and deliver exceptional customer service at every opportunity.

40. Learn the corporate culture, the company's story, and how the company functions and makes money. These are critical to connecting the dots to what you do and how it affects the bottom and top lines (revenue and expense).

41. Be proactive in seeking new assignments or job-enriching opportunities without the consistent expectation that you'll reap financial rewards or other perks—sometimes learning something new *is* the perk and can lead to financial rewards later in your career.

42. Save money, at least six months to one year of your annual salary.

43. Manage your reputation.

44. Avoid self-deprecating phrases such as, "That, oh, that was nothing," or "I know this may sound stupid, but…"

45. Seek approval when you need it, but not just to be liked. Hedge phrases such as, "Don't you agree?" or "I sort of…" or "What do you think?" make you appear less confident and reduce the impact of your communication.

46. Don't allow a bad boss or bad work scenario to keep you from being successful.

47. Properly develop relationships within the business unit and around the organization at various levels, not just in your age group, demographic group, or job level.

48. Practice proper etiquette: proper place settings, which fork to use, napkin on lap before eating, firm handshakes, eye contact, fresh breath, and clean smell. Be well groomed, stand tall, and articulate your words clearly.

49. Arrive five minutes early to every internal meeting—this is where relationships are established.

50. Be Resourceful. Find a way, an answer, or a solution to the challenge at hand, and you'll soon find yourself inside more circles than outside of them.

Watch your thoughts, for they become words.

Watch your words, for they become actions.

Watch your actions, for they become habits.

Watch your habits, for they become character.

Watch your character, for it becomes your destiny.

Bibliography

"Blog." *Wikipedia, the Free Encyclopedia*. Web. Spring 2011, http://en.wikipedia.org/wiki/Blog.

"Changes in the Workplace Reveal New Realities for Multigenerational Workforce." *World at Work*. 27 May 2008, www.worldatwork.org/waw/adimLink?id=26533.

Davies, John. "Credit Action - The National Money Education Charity | Welcome to Credit Action." *Credit Action - The National Money Education Charity | Welcome to Credit Action*. Www.creditaction.org.uk, Dec. 2012. Web. 14 Dec. 2012.

Florida State University. Informational Interviews. Raw data. Florida State University.

Fricker, Martin. "Scrooge Lives: Traffic Warden Tickets Two Ambulances Collecting Disabled Kids after Performing at Cha

Green, Pamela, and Society for Human Resource Management. "From Backpack to Briefcase." SHRM Regional Student Conference. Seattle, Washington. Winter 2010. Speech.

Groysberg, Boris, L. Kevin Kelly, and Bryan MacDonald. "The New Path to the C-Suite." *Harvard Business Review*. Mar. 2011: 60–68.

"Information Society." *Wikipedia, the Free Encyclopedia*, http://en.wikipedia.org/wiki/Information_society.

Karoly, Lynn A., and Constantijn W. A. Panis. *The 21st Century at Work: Forces Shaping the Future Workforce and Workplace in the United States.* Santa Monica, CA: RAND, 2004.

Lombardo, Michael M., and Robert W. Eichinger. *The Career Architect Development Planner: An Expert System Offering 95 Research Based and Experience Tested Development Plans and Coaching Tips for Learners, Supervisors, Managers, Mentors, and Feedback Givers.* Minneapolis, MN: Lominger, 2000.

ManpowerGroup. "Entering The Human Age: A New Era." *ManpowerGroup.* 15 June 2011, www.manpowergroup.com/humanage/entering-the-human-age.html.

Maxwell, John C., and Jim Dornan. *Becoming a Person of Influence: How to Positively Impact the Lives of Others.* Nashville, TN: T. Nelson, 1997.

Mig, Cat. "10 Benefits Of Networking." Made Manual. *Mademan.com*, www.mademan.com/mm/10-benefits-networking.html.

"Mish's Global Economic Trend Analysis: Canada Household Debt Approaches US Bubble Levels; Inane Housing Comments From Canadian Economist." *Mish's Global Economic Trend Analysis: Canada Household Debt Approaches US Bubble Levels; Inane Housing Comments From Canadian Economist.* N.p., 16 Oct. 2012. Web. 14 Dec. 2012.

Mooney, Kelly, and Laura Bergheim. "Introduction." *The Ten Demandments: Rules to Live by in the Age of the Demanding Consumer.* New York: McGraw-Hill, 2002, xiii—11.

Nguyen, Peter. "3 Types of Networking." *LinkedIn User Manual.* Talentelle.com, 5 Jan. 2007, http://linkedinusermanual.blogspot.com/2007/01/3-types-of-networking.html.

"Recruiting the Next Generation [Wandel Der Arbeitswelt]." *Recruiting the Next Generation,* www.recruitingthenextgeneration.de/index.php?article_id=34.

Sanders, Tim. *The Likeability Factor: How to Boost Your L-factor & Achieve Your Life's Dreams.* New York: Crown, 2005.

Schramm, Jennifer, Joseph Coombs, and Justina Victor. *SHRM Workplace Forecast—2011.* Alexandria: SHRM, 2011.

"Scrooge Lives: Traffic Warden Tickets Two Ambulances Collecting Disabled Kids after Performing at Charity Carol Concert." *Mirror.* N.p., n.d. Web. 19 Dec. 2012.

"A Service Economy." *America—Engaging the World.* America.gov Archive, 7 Apr. 2008, www.america.gov/st/econ-english/2008/April/20080415222038eaifas0.9101831.html.

Society for Human Resource Management and The Economist. *Global Firms in 2020—The Next Decade of Change for Organisations and Workers.* London: Rep. Economist Intelligence Unit Limited, 2010.

Wang, Jennifer, and Kara Ohngren. "The Disrupters: Forces Driving Change in 2011." *Entrepreneur,* 2 Dec. 2010, www.entrepreneur.com/article/printthis/217508.html.

We Are the First [user name]. "Preparing Your Business to Go Global." *Small Business Ideas,* 22 Nov. 2010, www.wearethe1s.org/small-business/preparing-your-business-to-go-global.

Williams, Gabrielle J. *The Making of a Young Entrepreneur.* Bowie: Legacy Builder Group, 2011.

Now What?

1. Visit our website: www.powerprojectinstitute.com:

   a. Subscribe to our free e-newsletter.

   b. Take the career assessment.

   c. Review our quality career resources.

2. Contact a power coach.

3. Join the Power Project community:

   a. Twitter: @PamelaJGreen

   b. Facebook: www.Facebook.com/PowerProjectInstitute

   c. LinkedIn: www.LinkedIn/in/PamelaJGreen

About the Author

First they ignore you, then they laugh at you,
then they fight you, and then YOU WIN!
~ Gandhi

Pamela J. Green is an engagement strategist, decisive thinker, and innovator of "Resourceful Leadership," a leadership technique that makes performers *want* to take responsibility for their problems, performance, and job satisfaction! Pamela has been featured in a multitude of media outlets, including *HR Magazine*, SHRM Online, *Associations Now*, *Biz Summits*, *The Columbus Post*, *The Network Journal*, the *Los Angeles Business Journal* and CSPNet.com.

A well-known figure in the HR world, popular keynote speaker, and notable business leader and power coach with over twenty-five years as a business leader for major brands like the American Red Cross, Head Start, and the Society for Human Resource Management, Pamela brings "big brand thinking" to small and medium-sized businesses. Her consultancy is focused on helping companies and associations attract and energize employees using specific strategies and techniques she has developed and implemented over her rich twenty-five years of leadership experience. She is also a highly sought after keynote speaker, author, and workshop facilitator, whose mission is to travel the world, teaching organizations and their employees how to be more productive and how to achieve phenomenal results.

Having experienced the good, the bad, and the very ugly in her own professional and personal life experiences, both as a leader and employee, she finds it therapeutic to share what she has learned with her clients and her audiences in a fun and highly engaging way. There is no way you will be able to walk away from an experience with Pamela without having one good belly laugh and learning something useful and practical for everyday use!

www.ingramcontent.com/pod-product-compliance
Lightning Source LLC
Chambersburg PA
CBHW060638210326
41520CB00010B/1659